MINI MAKERS

by Lauren Kukla

raintree
a Capstone company — publishers for children

Raintree is an imprint of Capstone Global Library Limited, a company incorporated in England and Wales having its registered office at 264 Banbury Road, Oxford, OX2 7DY – Registered company number: 6695582

www.raintree.co.uk
myorders@raintree.co.uk

Hardback edition © Capstone Global Library Limited 2024
Paperback edition © Capstone Global Library Limited 2025
The moral rights of the proprietor have been asserted.

All rights reserved. No part of this publication may be reproduced in any form or by any means (including photocopying or storing it in any medium by electronic means and whether or not transiently or incidentally to some other use of this publication) without the written permission of the copyright owner, except in accordance with the provisions of the Copyright, Designs and Patents Act 1988 or under the terms of a licence issued by the Copyright Licensing Agency, 5th Floor, Shackleton House, 4 Battle Bridge Lane, London, SE1 2HX (www.cla.co.uk). Applications for the copyright owner's written permission should be addressed to the publisher.

Edited by: Jessica Rusick
Designed by: Aruna Rangarajan, Sarah DeYoung
Originated by Capstone Global Library Ltd

ISBN 978 1 3982 5170 0 (hardback)
ISBN 978 1 3982 5171 7 (paperback)

British Library Cataloguing in Publication Data
A full catalogue record for this book is available from the British Library.

Acknowledgements
We would like to thank the following for permission to reproduce photographs: iStockphoto: avean (font), Front Cover, 1, Back Cover; Mighty Media, Inc.: 5 (pencil), project photos; Shutterstock: donatas1205, 5 (right), exopixel, Front Cover (jelly beans), Feng Yu, 5 (left), New Africa, 9 (refrigerator), TabitaZn, Back Cover (gift tag)

Design Elements: iStockphoto: Tolga TEZCAN; Shutterstock: ds_vector, Valerii_M

Every effort has been made to contact copyright holders of material reproduced in this book. Any omissions will be rectified in subsequent printings if notice is given to the publisher.

All the internet addresses (URLs) given in this book were valid at the time of going to press. However, due to the dynamic nature of the internet, some addresses may have changed, or sites may have changed or ceased to exist since publication. While the author and publisher regret any inconvenience this may cause readers, no responsibility for any such changes can be accepted by either the author or the publisher.

Printed and bound in India

CONTENTS

Mini gifts.. 4
Mini garden gnome 6
Mini wall hanging magnet................. 8
Mini gift basket 10
Mini succulent planters.................... 12
Mini lotion bars...................................... 14
Mini sushi toys.. 16
Mini envelope.. 18
Mini birthday card 20
Mini box of chocolates...................... 22
Mini jotting journal 24
Mini gift bag 28
   Find out more 32
   About the author........................... 32

MINI GIFTS

There's nothing better than a homemade gift to show someone you care. But what if that gift were small enough to fit in a pocket? Make someone's day with miniature gifts!

You could make a **teeny box of chocolates** for a friend with a sweet tooth.

Create a **mini succulent planter** or **tiny garden gnome** for your grandma with a green thumb.

Or give your mum a super-small spa experience with some **little lotion bars**.

Whatever you choose, these mini gift craft projects are bound to **SURPRISE** and **DELIGHT!**

BASIC SUPPLIES

- » coloured card
- » craft foam
- » felt
- » glue stick
- » hot-glue gun
- » marker pens
- » paint and paintbrush
- » ruler
- » scissors
- » scrapbook paper

Crafting tips

SET YOURSELF UP FOR SUCCESS! Read through the materials and instructions before starting a project. Cover your workspace with paper or plastic to protect it from messes or spills.

LET YOUR CREATIVITY SHINE! Put your own stamp on these projects. Don't be afraid to make changes or try something new!

UPCYCLE! Lots of the projects in this book use materials you'll probably find around your home. Is there something you can't find? Think of ways to adapt the project using items you do have.

ASK FIRST! Get permission to do the projects and to use any materials you find at home or school.

SAFETY FIRST! Ask an adult for help with projects that require sharp or hot tools.

CLEAN UP! When you've finished crafting, make sure you put away any supplies you took out. Clean up any spills and wipe down your crafting surface.

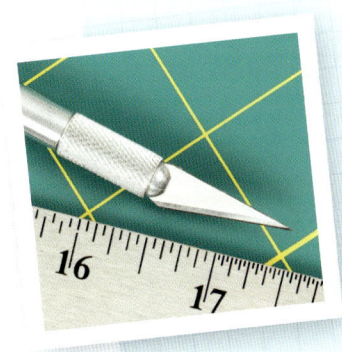

Mini GARDEN GNOME

MATERIALS

- » paint (colours of your choice) and paintbrushes
- » 2 mini terracotta pots, one slightly smaller than the other
- » 2 circular pebbles
- » 2 oval pebbles
- » hot-glue gun
- » wooden bead

This little gnome is perfect for a fairy garden or window box!

1

Paint the smaller terracotta pot and let it dry.

2

Paint the larger pot a different colour. This is the gnome's body. Leave space on the pot and paint a beard there. Let the paint dry.

3

Paint the two circular pebbles. They will be the gnome's shoes. Let the pebbles dry.

4

Paint the two oval pebbles to look like arms. Paint hands in any skin colour. Make the sleeves the same colour as the gnome's body.

5

Place the rim of the smaller pot over the bottom of the larger pot so it looks like a hat. Glue it in place.

6

Glue the arms and shoes to the larger pot.

7

If you like, paint the wooden bead the same colour as the gnome's skin. Glue the bead just below the edge of the smaller pot for the gnome's nose. Then give your gnome to a garden lover!

Mini WALL HANGING MAGNET

MATERIALS

- » card or scrapbook paper
- » ruler
- » scissors
- » felt-tip pens
- » wooden stir sticks
- » hot-glue gun
- » string
- » small magnet

Draw your own messages and doodles on these mini magnets!

1

Cut a rectangle of card or scrapbook paper that is 4 centimetres wide and 6 cm long.

2

Decorate the paper with a quote or drawing.

3

Cut two pieces of wooden stir sticks that are slightly wider than the paper. Glue them across the top and bottom edges of the paper.

4

Cut a piece of string 5 to 7.5 cm long. Glue the ends of the string to the top back corners of the paper.

5

Glue a small magnet to the back of the paper. Give your mini wall hanging magnet to a friend or loved one!

Mini GIFT BASKET

Fill this itty bitty basket with fun sweets and knick-knacks!

MATERIALS

- » small paper cup
- » craft knife
- » ruler
- » wooden stir sticks
- » scissors
- » hot-glue gun
- » bowl
- » warm water
- » little gifts, such as lip balm, sweets and knick-knacks

1

Using a craft knife, cut the top edge off the paper cup so the cup is about 4 cm tall.

2

Using scissors, cut several wooden stir sticks into 5-cm strips. Glue the strips vertically around the paper cup.

3

Cut several more stir sticks into 1.3-cm pieces. Glue them horizontally around the top and bottom of the basket.

4

Cut a 10-cm piece from a stir stick. Soak it in a bowl of warm water for 15 minutes. Gently bend the stick to form a basket handle. Glue the ends of the handle to the inside of the basket.

5

Fill the basket with little gifts!

Mini SUCCULENT PLANTERS

MATERIALS

» craft foam
» ruler
» scissors
» gold marker pen or gold paint and paintbrush
» plastic eggs
» hot-glue gun
» mini succulents (real or fake)
» potting soil

Bring colour and cheer to any window ledge with these mini planters!

1
Cut a triangle with 6-cm sides out of craft foam.

2
Colour or paint the craft foam gold and let it dry.

3
Pull apart a plastic egg and set aside the top half for a future project. Colour or paint the rim of the bottom half gold to match the craft foam.

4
Hot-glue the craft foam to the bottom of the egg.

5

Plant a mini succulent in potting soil in the egg-half.

6

Repeat steps 1 to 5 to make more mini planters!

Mini LOTION BARS

These marvellous mini lotion bars are the perfect gift for a friend who deserves some pampering!

MATERIALS

- » measuring cups
- » 120 millilitres shea butter or cocoa butter
- » 120 ml coconut oil
- » 120 ml beeswax
- » microwave
- » microwave-safe glass bowl
- » mixing spoon
- » essential oil (optional)
- » mini silicon moulds
- » string

1

Combine the shea or cocoa butter, coconut oil and beeswax in a bowl. Stir together.

2

Stir in 10 to 20 drops of essential oil, if you like.

3

Microwave on high for 30-second bursts, stirring between each one, until the mixture has completely melted.

4

Spoon the mixture into the silicon moulds. Set aside to cool and harden.

5

Pop the bars out. Stack two or three bars together and tie them with string for a pretty presentation!

Mini SUSHI TOYS

MATERIALS
- » marker pen
- » felt
- » scissors
- » ruler
- » hot-glue gun
- » cotton balls
- » puffy fabric paint

These tiny toys will make cute and cuddly buddies for a friend or sibling!

1
Draw two identical triangles on a piece of felt. Cut them out.

2
Hot-glue the triangles together, leaving a 2.5-to-5-cm gap.

3
Pull the triangle inside out.

> **TINY TIP**
> Instead of sushi, make toys of your friend's favourite food, like pizza or a hot dog!

4

Pull apart cotton balls and use them to stuff the triangle. Glue along the gap to close it.

5

Repeat steps 1 to 4 with other shapes to make more sushi toys. Then use puffy fabric paint and felt pieces to decorate them!

17

Mini ENVELOPE

MATERIALS
- » coloured card
- » ruler
- » scissors
- » pencil
- » glue stick

A super-small envelope is the perfect holder for a tiny note or card!

1

Cut a square piece of coloured card 5 cm by 5 cm.

2

Draw a vertical and horizontal line through the middle of the square, dividing it into four equal parts.

3

Fold two opposite corners to the centre.

4

Draw a horizontal line on one unfolded corner, about 0.5 cm above the centre point.

5

Fold along the line to make the bottom flap of the envelope.

6

Fold the point of the bottom flap and tuck it inside the envelope. Trim the point of the top flap to round it.

7

Glue the bottom flap in place. Fold down the top flap to finish your envelope!

TINY TIP
Use the ruler as a straight edge to make sure your lines are perfectly straight!

Mini BIRTHDAY CARD

MATERIALS

» coloured card (plain, various patterns and colours)

» ruler

» scissor

» pencil

» glue stick

The teeny tiny cake inside this card makes an adorable pop-up birthday surprise!

1

Cut a 12.5 × 7.5-cm rectangle out of patterned card. Cut a 11 × 6-cm rectangle out of plain card.

2

Fold the plain card in half. Draw a 4-cm line near the bottom of the card, perpendicular to the fold. Draw a second, identical line 2.5 cm away from the first. Draw a third line 4 cm away from the second line. Make it 2.5 cm long.

3

Cut along the lines. Fold the card along the fold in the opposite direction to pop out two strips. These will be the cake's layers.

4

Cut strips of card the same length and width as the cake layers. Glue them onto the cake.

5

Cut several candles and flames out of card. The candles should be about 2.5 cm long by 0.5 cm wide. Glue the flames to the candles. Then glue the candles to the cake.

6

Open the plain card and centre it behind the patterned card rectangle. Glue in place and fold the card in half to finish it!

Mini BOX OF CHOCOLATES

MATERIALS

- » empty matchbox
- » tissue paper
- » scissors
- » paperboard
- » chocolate chunks
- » knife and cutting board
- » white chocolate chips
- » butterscotch chips
- » scrapbook paper or coloured card
- » glue stick
- » marker pen

Fill this tiny chocolate box with delicious mini treats!

1

Cut a piece of tissue paper to fit inside the matchbox. The piece of tissue paper can be a little longer than the matchbox.

2

Cut two narrow strips of paperboard the same length as the matchbox. Place them inside the matchbox to create dividers for the chocolates.

3

Cut chocolate chunks into small squares of chocolate.

4

Place the chocolate squares in the matchbox with white chocolate chips and butterscotch chips.

5

Cut a piece of scrapbook paper or coloured card the size of the matchbox cover. Glue the paper onto the cover.

6

Write "chocolate" on the paper. Or write a sweet message for the recipient!

Mini JOTTING JOURNAL

MATERIALS

- » paper
- » ruler
- » scissors
- » 2 binder clips
- » hot-glue gun
- » pencil
- » cardboard
- » craft knife
- » coloured card
- » fabric

Make a pocket-sized journal for taking notes on the go! Give it to a friend who loves to write or draw.

1

Cut 20 rectangles of paper that are 7.5 × 5 cm.

2

Fold each rectangle in half. Stack them so the folded ends face the same direction. Put a binder clip on both short ends of the stack.

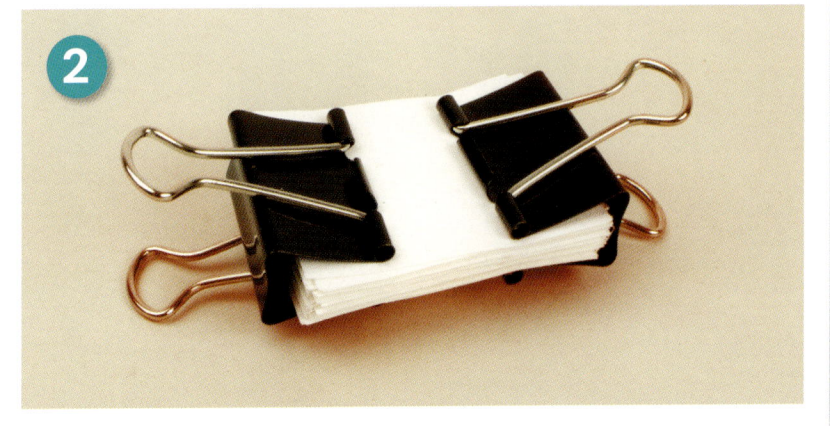

3

Hot-glue along the folded edges to secure the journal's pages.

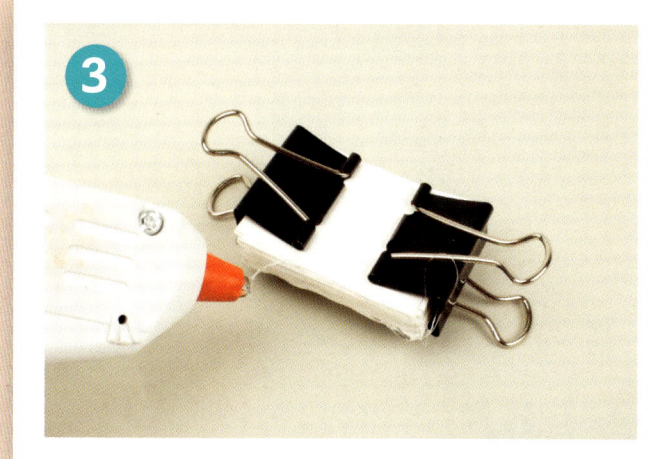

4

Cut a 10 × 5-cm piece of cardboard. This will be the journal's cover.

5

Draw a line 4 cm in from each short end to mark where the journal's binding will go.

TINY TIP

Cardboard is made of layers. To score cardboard, use a craft knife to slice through just a few of the layers. This allows you to make a flap that folds and unfolds easily!

CONTINUED ON THE NEXT PAGE »

6

Use a craft knife to score along each line. Fold at the lines to make the cover.

7

Cut a piece of card slightly smaller than the cover. Glue it to the cover's inside.

8

Cut a piece of fabric about 1.5 cm bigger than the cover on each side. Centre the outer cover in the fabric and glue in place.

9

Glue the excess fabric to the inside cover.

26

10

Glue the journal pages to the cover's inner spine. Leave it to dry. Your journal is ready!

Mini GIFT BAG

MATERIALS
- » scrapbook or origami paper
- » ruler
- » scissors
- » glue stick
- » string
- » hot-glue gun
- » tissue paper (optional)

Make a miniature bag to hold all your tiny gifts!

1
Cut a 7.5 × 10-cm paper rectangle.

2
Fold the rectangle in half widthwise and open it again.

3
Fold the left half of the rectangle to meet the centre crease line.

4
Fold the right half so it overlaps the left half by 0.5 to 1.5 cm. Glue down the overlapped portion with a glue stick. Fold up one short end of the bag 2.5 cm to make the bottom flap.

5

Open the bottom flap, pressing the left and right sides down as you do. This will make a diamond shape.

6

Fold the top flap of the diamond down, making a crease about 1.5 cm from the diamond's centre. Unfold.

TINY TIP
Use your fingernail or a craft stick to firmly crease each fold you make.

CONTINUED ON THE NEXT PAGE »

7

Fold the diamond's bottom flap up to meet the crease from step 6. Glue it in place. Glue the top flap to the bottom flap to make the bottom of the bag.

8

Fold the right edge of the bag in so it meets the bottom triangle. Repeat on the left side.

9

Open the bag. Re-crease the folds on the left side so the crease goes in the opposite direction. Repeat on the other side.

10

Cut two pieces of string about 4 cm long. Put two dots of hot glue on one top, inside edge of the bag. Stick the ends of a piece of string onto each dot to make a handle. Repeat on the other side to make a second handle.

11

If you like, cut strips of tissue paper. Use them to stuff your bag!

FIND OUT MORE

BOOKS

10-Minute Crafty Projects (10-Minute Makers), Elsie Olson (Raintree, 2022)

Spring Crafts From Different Cultures (Multicultural Seasonal Crafts), Megan Borgert-Spaniol (Raintree, 2023)

The Repair Shop Craft Book, Sònia Albert (Walker, 2023)

WEBSITES

www.bbc.co.uk/cbeebies/makes/lets-go-club-ten-minute-crafts?collection=the-lets-go-club-craft-activities
The CBeebies website has lots of quick craft activities to do.

www.goodhousekeeping.com/home/craft-ideas/g39762537/crafts-for-kids/
Find ideas for some easy craft activities on this website.

ABOUT THE AUTHOR

Lauren Kukla is a poet and an author of books and media for children. She loves embroidery, walking, camping and growing vegetables in her garden. She lives with her husband, two small children, a silly white dog and four city chickens in Minneapolis, Minnesota, USA. You can follow her poetry on Instagram @NorthCountryPoet.